The Left Side of Grace

by
CYNTHIA ATKINS

TITLE:
The Left Side of Grace

AUTHOR:
Cynthia Atkins

PUBLISHED BY:
Cynthia Atkins

EDITOR:
Dr. R L Stevenson Sr
Prinnies Moore

ISBN:
978-1-947574-86-1

PRINTED IN THE UNITED STATES OF AMERICA

Copyright © 2025 Cynthia Atkins

All rights reserved. This book is copyright material and must not be copied, reproduced, transferred, distributed, leased, licensed or used in any way except as specifcally permitted in writing by the author, as allowed under the terms and conditions under which it was purchased or as strictly permitted by applicable copyright law. Respective authors own all copyrights not held by the publisher.In no way is it legal to reproduce, duplicate, or transmit any part of this document in either electronic means or printed format.

Any unauthorised distribution or use of this text may be a direct infringement of the Author's rights, and those responsible may be liable in law accordingly.

DEDICATION

This book is dedicated to the memory of Clifford and Audrey Caldwell-my grandparents.

INTRODUCTION

And the word was made flesh, and dwelt among us, (and we beheld his glory, the glory as of the only begotten of the Father,) full of grace and truth.
John 1:14.

TABLE OF CONTENTS

Chapter 1: The Baptism

11

Chapter 2: A Charge to Keep

25

Chapter 3: Graveyard Story

37

Chapter 4: These Rocks Got No Names

51

Chapter 5: Bringing the Bones

59

Chapter 6: The Left Side of Grace

97

Chapter 7: Quartet Singers Ain't Never Been No Good

111

CHAPTER 1:
The Baptism

Sunrise in Fairbanks, Mississippi spilled through the Leary's backyard on a rooster's crow. No matter the season, that bird knows the exact time the Lord was ready to stop playing possum. The garden out back broke ground with fresh collards, tomatoes and green peppers. Sugar cane rods were hollowed out and its solid sprouts crossed, supporting rows of hanging green beans high as the back outhouse creating privacy from the Jones place that loomed across the creek.

Rows of cabbage and white potatoes grew ripe in the earth, while plum trees, dropped bittersweet treats over the fence of hedges in the front yard. Everybody on Taylor Street knew the Leary's land was rich and fertile.

Ed and Idell Leary, my grandparents, worked the land for twenty years, as Grandpa told it, and each summer season the back garden was a proud source of food. He took pride in the seeding and self-irrigation of the land that fed many families without them having to ask.

All it took was a compliment of "Those show are some good-looking collards, Ed" and before you knew it, the charmer was walking off with a bunch.

But the earth was its own after a certain hour on the night, so some folks took to gathering vegetables after dark. It saved their pride in some marvelous fashion to steal at the glow of the lightning bugs rather than ask. Grandpa would often say He'd rather "Root Hog and Die Po" before he put himself in such a predicament.

This Saturday, mid morning, I watched from behind the string beans, a knobby knee, ten year old, while Grandpa Leary scratched his head and swore over the worms that pilfered two rows of cabbage. The tiny holes peeping through the leafage was making mockery of the white homemade pesticide Grandpa concocted that sprinkled over everything green planted in the deep-rooted rows of vegetables.

I didn't mind the spoiling of the cabbage so much. After Grandma smothered them with two slabs of smoke house salt pork and her perfect dash of salt, I usually ended up with an awful case of the gas.

It was such a dinner on that Saturday night that had my stomach in knots until the wee hours of morning. The shadows out back were kept company by my traipsing back and forth from the bed to the outhouse and it wasn't until old rooster Joe crowed that I knew for sure the night was over.

Grandma had already left for church riding along with Mrs. Jones since both had early kitchen duties and Deacon Jones had early door opening duties and the like…but I was slow to respond to any sense of urgency Grandpa had about rising for Sunday morning worship.

It was still dark out and grandpa barely gave me time to wash before dragging the gown over my head and carrying me out the door. I was too sleepy to tell him he left my shoes but was certain Grandma would point it out.

Through drooping eyes, I saw him glancing at his pocket

watch, "It's ten past eight," he muttered to himself.

The desperate way he maneuvered the curves in the road was a clear indication that we were running late. It made the ride to the church quick and the back window was cracked just enough to catch any passing breeze from the speed of the car without messing up my bangs. The back seat of the Chrysler seemed deeper this day because I was forced to sit in the seat instead of leaning over the back chatting with grandpa about every turn in the road. It took weeks to bring me to this moment and grandpa was wasting no more time in making sure I got to the church. He said dressing himself and keeping up with a youngen was more than he bargained for without Grandma hustling about.

My toes gripped the back seat of the Chrysler in a desperate attempt at bracing against the sudden turns and I felt relief when the car finally bumped across the gravel church parkway, sliding noisily past the line of worshipers, next to the pastor's car, which was the usual spot for the chairman of the deacon board to park.

"Lisa, git on out now and get in line like you suppose to," said grandpa, before the car could come to, what I thought, was a full stop.

I used both hands to release the handle of the door.

"Grandpa, I don't think I'm suppose to wear my gown in. I think I'm supposed to put it on when I get inside."

"Don't matter. Get in line like you suppose to, folks already lining up."

So… I hurried towards the back door of the church to join the line of singing marchers. A frantic Deacon Jones was standing there holding it open as smoke spilled past him. The smell of burnt chicken filled the air. A hand holding a black smoking skillet hung out the window alongside the door. I could tell that hand anywhere. It was Grandmas.

Before I could think to look around for Grandpa, I felt someone push me firmly in line, like a slow rehearsed dance.

Most of Saturday was spent with Grandma ringing the necks of four of Grandpa's best yard birds. I watched from the top step of the Porch in fascination as she cornered each of them. Their headless Bodies scurrying about- no different than before Grandma caught them.

It seemed the whole day was spent getting ready for Baptismal Sunday. Grandma said it was biggest coming to Jesus celebration on this side of the state of Mississippi.

"Most Folks don't see this much goings on in a church unless a preacher dies," She chuckled, as she cut the chicken into pieces.

It seemed a shame to see those chickens come to such a dark end, I thought.

I pulled at the collar of my white cotton gown. Grandma made the gown especially for me and the embroidery on the collar came from the exact dress my own mother wore on her special day. It didn't feel so special though, more scratchy than anything else.

The smoke was clearing up and I could feel grandma's eyes piercing through me from the back kitchen window of the church but I dared not turn around to confirm it. She was on kitchen duty this Sunday but her eyes still had the power to reach across the yard and chastise you if needed.

The special lace that circled the neck of my grown was digging into my collar bone like the mosquitoes were digging into my ankles. I didn't know whether to scratch my neck or risk bending over and scratching my ankles.

Grandma was a stickler about behaving properly, especially at church, so I dare not be the one stooped over holding up the line.

The line was moving slowly and I could see a sea of white dresses in front of me. All the girls were lined up according to age. First the twelve year old's, then the eleven year olds, until the last group, my group, the ten year olds. We all stood quietly, the morning wind sliding through our smartly ironed gowns- bare feet sinking through the grass, still cool with dew untouched by the sun. The grass was the only comfort and I made a game of capturing the blades between my toes.

I also discovered my feet were the perfect weapon to slap the annoying bugs from my ankles. I tugged at the collar again, and peered around the girl in front of me, hoping to get a glimpse of the pool of water that was normally hidden underneath a tin top in the back of New Hope Baptist Church. I had never seen the outside pond because the deacons kept it covered with that tin. It was in a far off corner in the back yard of the church. You had to walk through the gravesite to reach it.

The Church itself stood on concrete blocks that made it easy for me to peer under it and see clear cross to the back. I was just tall enough to play under the Church without bumping my head on the floor beams. The back stairs led a path to the stagnate pool of water and I'd walked that path many Sunday mornings after Sunday school.

I would throw rocks at the black water bugs that scampered towards it until it was time for morning devotion.

This Sunday, standing in line waiting my turn, I couldn't help but wonder where the water bugs got off to this day.

There was no sign of them anywhere.

The line moved again and I was able to see the women of the Mother Board and Ushers circled around the pool with their white uniforms and fans waving. Their faces shimmered with sweat and their voices sang out a tune that brought action.

"Take me to the water, take me to the water, take me to the water, to be baptized."

The only time there was a lull in the singing was when Pastor

Surry's voice rang out to Jesus.

"I'm gonna baptize you in the name of the Father, In the name of the Son, In the name of the Holy Ghost…Three in One."

Then the ladies in white would start up the song again. The more they sang the quicker the line moved until my feet were no longer on the grass but on the asphalt that surrounded the pool.

The grit beneath my feet seemed to be the very thing that scared the mosquitoes away. The moisture from the grass was replaced with the moisture that spilled from the baptismal pool side.

I was next… but I couldn't get myself to move any closer To the circle of women. I couldn't get my feet to move toward the booming Pastor Surry. I looked around again towards the kitchen window, hoping grandma would say, "It's ok if you don't want to."

She was in the window all right. The scowl on her face said, "Git Your tail in that water before I have to come out there." It was the same look I got that night during revival when it was time for the doors of the church to be opened. That meant it was time to come up front, if you had not already and proclaim the Lord Jesus as your savior.

My grandparents had already talked to me about it. Grandma huffed,

"When Pastor opens the doors of the Church, you go up there this time. It's time for you to get baptized."

I knew to do as I was told, so when Pastor Surry said,

"I don't know about you but Jesus---He's been good to me…
I said Jesus, Mary's baby---He's been so good to me…

Am I right about it? If he's been good to you…You oughta tell Somebody!

I don't know about you but he's like fire…shut up in My bones!

He's My Way-maker, My Heavy load sharer, My Burden Barrier. My Rock in a weary land!

Won't he hold you? Won't he wipe your Tears away?

So I say RIGHT NOW!…RIGHT NOW is the Time…

You know Death comes…Death comes like a Thief in the night! Don't let him catch you with your work undone…

Come on Sinner!

Come on ole wretched, tired soul!

Whosoever come, come…The doors of the church are open!"

I looked up to find Grandma looking me dead in the eye from the Mother board corner. It was time to "come to Jesus."

I slipped off the pew and walked to the man with his arms out stretched-me and fifteen other mindless girls. I knew all I had to say was "Yes" to anything asked. Grandma had told me that much too.

She didn't tell me about next part though. Nobody had. Not even Grandpa and I relied on him to tell me everything. He was the only one that told what happened to my Mother and why my Daddy let them raise me. He was the one that showed me how to play without my shoes on and still keep from stubbing my toe. He didn't tell why they kept this pool covered or even how deep it was. He didn't tell where the bugs had gone.

The singing from the women rose high above my head. I turned again looking up at the women in white. I looked over at the dripping girls before me with gowns clinging limp like to their bodies. Their mothers were there waiting on the other side with a towel in hand waiting to drain the water from their hair first, then their gowns ,while hurrying them off back down the path.

A warm feeling came over me and I felt my throat tighten; my toes planted themselves solidly and my arms fell by my side.

A voice came from the other side of Pastor Surry, "Come on child," it said coaxingly. I looked up to see Grandpa moving through the water around Pastor Surry with his hands reaching out.

"Come on child, I got cha." He looked bigger than anything did at that moment. He looked bigger than the water. He looked bigger than the singing mothers that stood by the pool.

He reached for me and all I felt was his hand on my elbows passing me effortlessly to Pastor Surry, whose words were muted. All I heard and all I saw was the big man in the corner of the deep pool of water. I saw him before I was immersed and after I was brought back into the light. He was there, grabbing my elbows and he placed me safely on the other side. He carried me to Grandma, still waiting in the church kitchen window. She had a smile so proud. I sat in the kitchen with my head covered in Grandma's best, company coming towel, only my wet bangs peeping out of the corners, eating fried chicken and sweet potato pie.

I thought…If coming to Jesus felt like this, I would come to him again next Sunday.

CHAPTER 2:
A Charge to Keep

The charge of the Leary's was to stay after church until business was handled. Since Grandpa was chairman, he had to total all monies after the end of Sunday service and Grandma was head of the kitchen even though that job had no title, folks just knew she was over things by the way she met you at the church kitchen door, haughty and expectant of compliments from the aroma of cornbread, collards, and chicken frying ... crackling in a mess of flour and lard.

Baptism Sunday meant nothing different.

A scowl crossed her face when she realized I had no change of clothes. My gown dried itself quickly by the heat of the stove but sweat replaced the dripping water so I smelled of fried food and musk by the time she finished with her kitchen duties. She paid no mind to me after a while which convinced me we had the church to ourselves except for Grandpa's voice rising from the pastor's study.

I wandered into the sanctuary, a forbidden boundary after service, just to feel the floor under my feet. The pulpit that loomed over the church pews looked cold, abandoned, and evil without fanning worshipers.

A ripping sound echoed, and I looked up to find Deacon Otis Jones tearing a banner from the back of the church pulpit.

The "He Lives" sign had served it's purpose. He didn't see me standing by the borders of the piano and I was shocked at the lack of care he exhibited. The festivities were over and the smell of burnt chicken was the last remaining evidence that anything went awry.

Deacon Otis was not tall enough to snatch the banner on his own. His small frame, perched on the choir bench, rocked back and forth violently at the suddenness of his own movement. Despite my best attempt, a laugh escaped my lips. He swung around suddenly which stopped my snickering, so I dropped my eyes fixing them on my toes.

"What chu in here for?", the Deacon muttered, looking behind me for an absent accompaniment.

"Waiting on Grandpa. I was looking for Mandy."

"Mandy better be off with her Mama, which is where you ought to be." His reference to me being off with my Ma seemed to disturb him more than it affected me.

"I mean off with your Granny," He clarified.

"She's wiping down the kitchen, sir. I best get back to helping her."

I still wanted to know what happened with Mandy. She was my best friend. We played jack stones with rocks and jump board with bricks. Since the Jones's lived across the creek, we would meet up in Grandpa's Garden and bite the sweet tomatoes. Grandpa never said anything which contributed to our acts of mischief.

Deacon Jones tapped his fingers on his forehead as if making a mental note of all things he had triple checked. I heard him say, "the Sanctuary is clean and the bibles are back in the book rack, the banner is down. I'll check the kitchen."

"Grandma will make sure the stove's off," I added.

The deacon turned in surprise making claim to the obvious. "I make sure everything turned off young lady, thank God for

Jesus, or this Church would of burned down like many before it."

I wanted to say the Church burnings had nothing to do with chicken left on the stove but thought better of it after Deacon Jones pushed past me. He walked quickly to the kitchen, and I followed like a help mate. His small hands checked all the buttons on the stove.

"It's off I told you."

Deacon Jones glanced impatiently across his shoulder and quickly walked over to the window aside the stove. They were all closed and secured. He checked the lights…they were out. "Where's your grandma, gurl?"

"I suppose she is helping Grandpa count the collections by now," I answered, wiping my hand across the table. The plastic tablecloth was still wet from Grandma's rag and the moisture from my hand left a small imprint that I transferred to my exposed thigh.

"Where's Mandy?" I asked again.

Deacon Jones scampered around the corner and Grandma's voice rang out, "Watch your holy feet on those hall flooring. I ain't giving no once overs today," she said, moving through the hallway like an avenging black angel.

"Just need to check the back-door locks, Mother Leary. There's a storm coming and we all know what happened last time the doors were left half open."

It was the best Sunday school ever because a tree snake was the opening introduction to Sister Mae's Sunday school class with ten other tiny members looking on. It took five minutes for Sister to report to Deacon Leary, who made it the new business topic at Tuesday's Deacon board meeting. Grandpa said you would have thought Lucifer himself showed up for Sunday school the way they carried on.

Leaving that door ajar almost cost Deacon Jones his charge and it did not help none that he could not recollect a thing about securing it.

From that day on, Grandpa said, Deacon Jones, started treating his janitor duties like his insurance collecting. He started writing stuff down.

I watched him walk over to his car parked at the end of the drive. There was no special parking for the custodian deacon and since he was there before anybody every Sunday anyway, there didn't seem to be a need.

Opening and closing had been a Jones duty for over twenty years let Deacon Jones tell it. For twenty years, he touted, "I see them coming and I see them going."

It was such a claim that got him keys to every door in the church, including the Pastor study.

I stood at the back door and watched him climb into the driver's seat of his station wagon. He reached for something under the passenger's side seat, pulled a pen from his dress pocket and began scribbling. I could see Mrs. Jones slumped over on her side…catching a nap while waiting…I didn't see Mandy…and I still wondered where she got off to.

The dust on the road had settled from the departing church folks by the time Grandpa was done with his charge. Only the crickets witnessed our slow crawl home. The ride home was slower. Grandpa and Grandma kept a steady conversation going about nothing particularly. It seemed to satisfy them both, one really did not have to answer the other. Anything I was not to hear was normally spelled out by Grandma who less than often got it right.

I was sent to bed quite early due to the day's excitement and rightly so. My head barely hit the pillow before slipping off to cricket land. It would have remained that way until morning except for the whispering on the porch.

It stirred me.

"Idell?"

I crawled across the bed towards the window, listening.

"Idell, Honey?" It was Grandpa.

"Hun?"
Grandma wasn't answering.

"Do me a favor?" he turned towards her, waiting.

"What Ed?" she finally replied.

"Before I die, will you sleep with me?"

I saw Grandma's back straighten. I pushed passed the pillows, inching even closer.

"There was a time it was OK, wasn't it?" He leaned closer to her.
"We were good with each other."

I waited to hear what would be said next. I thought surely they would hear me through the window behind them.

Grandma rose to her feet.

"You can't keep putting it out of your mind," he continued.
"Shut up!" She snapped." Don't start talking in my clothes, not now."
I knew that meant Grandpa wanted to touch Grandma's private spot and Grandma told me never let nobody talk in your clothes

and try to touch your private spot.

"It ain't that. I just want to hear you," he said quietly.

The silence that followed was deafening.

"What are you listening for, Ed?"

"Just you," he responded.

"I want to hear you resting …One last time."

She turned to him, her face was wet.

"Resting?" she frowned, wiping her face.

"You ain't heard ME resting…You heard me running."

He leaned back in the chair.

"I thought if I laid there, just still enough. You'd soon do the same," she said softly.

"I just couldn't stand your hands no more…grabbing at me." Grandpa wasn't moving.

"I gave you nine chirren, Ed. Course you might just count eight. I'm full of baby…nine times", she forgot to whisper.

"Don't remember even taking a breath between em. None of em. Belly so big, couldn't see my own feet standing up, for nine years. Sarah being the last…"

Sarah. That was my mother's name.

"I did all I knew to do." He groaned.

"I worked, I tried, Sarah just…"

"Sarah just what?" She responded, holding her stomach, "I don't recall the good about it, Ed." She said, looking at his bowed head.

"Goddamn me for that."
That was one of the few times I ever heard Grandma curse. It made my heart pound through my throat.

Grandma walked softly through the porch door and in the bedroom.

"Lisa?" she called.

I pretended to be asleep.

CHAPTER 3:
Graveyard Story

Honeysuckles grew wild through the fence of hedges along the front of the house. The sweet scent was the first clue that it was morning. It crept through the cracked window on a draft, making my sweat soaked pillow a cooling board.

I could see the blossoms from where I lay. Early morning was the best time to taste them, before the road dust settled on the blooms. I wished I was in the yard amongst them, if only to taste the dewy drops hiding inside the yellow buds. Instead, I lay silently, watching the sun create a shadow across the bed. I was as still as a mouse in the eyesight of a hawk-shaking but paralyzed. Numbness invaded my limbs. If I did not move soon, I felt my body would surely crack.

Grandma laid on the other side of me. Her broad back stopping the ray of sun in its tracks. Her breathing had a haunting steadiness. I could feel it like it was coming from my own body. I counted the rasping sound, waiting on her to wake up. I knew to wait. The wetness between my legs was beginning to smell. My sleep too deep to stop the liquid trail that snaked through the sheets at some time during the wee hours. It was a shame I bore for two years now. I held my breath as I moved my left hand behind my back, feeling for the hem of Grandma's nightdress.

It felt tangled and to my horror, had found a place just under my legs to hide. I pressed my fingers against the fabric of the gown. It was as damp as the mattress beneath it.

All the excitement from Sunday must have been too much for me, I thought. Grandma said I only wet the bed when I got excited and getting excited made me lazy. That did not make much sense to me. It was exciting to have ice cream and sweet tea on the front porch and watching them just being quiet with each other-until Grandma sent me off to bed.

Last night I opened my eyes after Grandma drifted off to rest. It was midnight dark in the room. Not even the moon cast a shadow. Grandpa's back was still blocking my view of the porch. I watched until he came in and walked grimly through the bedroom only pausing to look over at me. I did not pretend to see him even though I knew he could not see my eyes. I wiggled my feet ever so slightly. That was our signal. It meant Goodnight. Me and Grandpa had many signals. It came in handy when it was not a good time for talking.

I watched him go back to the back room. That's what Grandama called his room. I called it the sky room because that's what his bed seemed to touch. I felt grand when I played on it, but I was never allowed to sleep there. Grandma said it just wasn't proper. I suppose that was why Grandma didn't sleep there as well. My sleeping spot was in Grandma's bed. I slept next to the window in the summer and next to the fireplace in the winter. Grandma said it was to keep me from setting up pneumonia.

Old Rooster Joe crowed and the shift in the bed made me stiffen. Grandma was turning towards the window. I heard her catch her breath and before she could say a word, I confessed the obvious.

"I done peed."

My voice was low but I knew I was heard. Grandma slid uneasily from the bed. Snatching the sheets and covers with her. I fell to the floor from the suddenness of it. Scampering to my feet, I backed away, until my back was touching the brick of the fireplace.

"Go on and get me what I need," Grandma said, peeling the wet clothes from her frame. I walked to the corner of the room and retrieved the Switch from behind the vanity. Last time she at least let me put on dry bloomers. A whipping was something awful when your bloomers were wet. The Switch loomed over my head. It was the third one this week. The others were thrown amongst the hedges out front, back to where they were stripped from-worn weak because Grandma also used them for swatting flies.

I handed the frayed branch to her with one hand and held the other hand in front of my knees. It normally started with the legs and if I cried quick enough, it would only last about five swats. As quick as lightning, the green branch swooped from the ceiling slicing across my ankles. My scream traveled clear to the back of the house. Grandpa's appearance in the door confirmed it.

"You just gone make her nervous if you keep that up," he muttered. "You go get yourself cleaned up," he demanded, turning to me.

"Don't you move!" Grandma stated, throwing the wet sheets at my feet.

"You got some cleaning here to do."

I didn't know whether to turn towards the bed to grab the soiled items or run to the door where Grandpa stood, so I laid in the floor waiting for his wordless signal. My ankles separated my body from the wood floor of the bedroom- the hardness unmerciful to the fresh sting of welt marks that circled past my shins. Tear soaked hands soothed the heated wounds that seem to spring up from my bones.

"The child got to learn there are consequences to her actions," Grandma said slowly, pulling the housecoat from the bedpost, covering herself. "There are consequences," she repeated. I wasn't sure what that meant.

"I think she knows that by now, She feels it," Grandpa said. "Do you understand me?" He walked over grabbing the Switch from her hand.

"She feels it when she's too slow about the cleaning, too fast about gathering eggs, too lazy to get to the outhouse…she feels your consequences."

The meaning was clearer now. It's what happens when you mess up. I watched Grandma turn to the closet pulling bedding from the top shelf and a small sheet of plastic.

"I suppose I am not surprised. You got a weakness in you Ed," she said.

She straddled the bed and laid the plastic sheet over the damp portion of the mattress. Her firm hands tossed the bed sheets across smoothing them in kind.

"It's all the same," she said, tackling her task. "It's all the same, she gone be just like her Ma. I guess that's what you want.

Yes Lawdy…that's what you want," She huffed.

"Who else she gone be like if not her Ma," Grandpa shot back. There were no words as Grandma finished making the bed. She walked past me, scooping the soiled sheets off the floor placing them on the vanity.

"You want to hear her screaming too, Ed? You ain't satisfied with screams of one child's voice in your ears?"

"I already told you how I found her," Grandpa said, shaking his head.

It was as though they forgot I was there on the floor, ankles throbbing from the weight of my body.

"I know what you said. You say a lot of things but then you ain't really said nothing when you think about it," she responded.

"Lisa, you go get yourself cleaned up like I told you," Grandpa said over his shoulder.

I didn't want to leave. What did it mean she was screaming? He said my Ma and Jesus kept me a secret until it was time for me to come into the world. He said it was a sweet secret and My Ma was lucky to be in cahoots with the Lord on it. He found her right after I was birthed.

"You was the prettiest thing I ever laid eyes on," He'd said.

"Grinning and shining on a crib bed of grass."

Nothing said about screaming.

"There's a rag and soap in the back," he prodded, gently. "You get to it."

I rose and stepped timidly towards Grandma, taking the wet sheets carefully with me. I walked through the door into the hallway past Grandpa's room to the back porch. I poured a good helping of water in the bowl from the churn vase that Grandma kept full. Goose bumps covered my body as I wiped pee from my bottom and legs, wincing when the water trickled to my ankles, reminding me of the giant switch and that I had no clean bloomers. I grabbed a larger towel, that dangled from the nail on the back door, wrapping it around my body and crept quietly back towards the bedroom. I could hear them from the hallway.

"I see you when I tell her things," Grandma said. "I watch how she clings to you even when I don't move."

I lingered in the hallway. If Grandma figured out their signals then there would be more consequences coming. My ankles could barely stand that. I walked into the bedroom almost tripping over the bottom of the towel.

"I forgot my bloomers."

Grandma looked at me like she had never looked at me before... then paused... and walked over to the chest of drawers. She retrieved a pair of white cotton bottoms shaking them as if she expected something to fall from them.

She pulled the towel away and stooped low enough for me to step into the bloomers while leaning on her shoulders. I started to pull away but was stopped by firm hands that circled the cheekbones of my face. I never remembered Grandma touching me like that. There was no fussing over a snotty nose or chastising over sleep filled eyes. The hands were gentle and still.

"When I was this child's age, My Ma taught me to pray. I told her ...I said... it just ain't coming to me natural. She knew it though...My Ma was good with me that way-always watching. She would say, "Idell-there are things you speak about and things you take to your grave." When I had my babies, I only spoke about it to the Lord. I felt only pain,no joy. I prayed ... cause I felt closed and disappointed. It was a taught prayer." She stood up lifting me to the bed.

"By the time Sarah came, after so much praying, I had just grown tired. I think that got God's attention. He wanted me to cry out and that just wasn't natural for me."

She turned to Grandpa.

"I have tried to understand how Sarah got by me?" She walked to the chest of drawers again, pulling out a pair of my Overalls. "I do all the washing in this house…but her condition…it got by me. A Mother is suppose to tell those kinds of things with a girl child."

The britches dangled from her waiting hand, and Grandpa walked over to grab it. She closed her fist firmly around the suspenders.

"If you found my child any other way, then what you say, then before God, I don't want to ever hear tell of it. If you were there…if you knew about it-you best make that your graveyard story."

She walked from the bedroom leaving silence for company. It took Grandpa a while to finish dressing me after Grandma left.

I suppose it was because he was shaking.

Monday morning seemed to stretch on forever. I crawled back on the bed fully clothed and listened to Grandma make breakfast. I could hear the water boiling for coffee and could picture her kneading the bread for hot biscuits...not even the smell of salt pork frying moved my appetite.

I could even hear Grandpa reading the paper out loud... muttering through the articles while Grandma pretended not to listen. She said he read out loud all the time cause it was a habit...said he read everything to his Ma and brothers as a child because they never took up learning, so he just never let it go. I didn't mind it so much. Some of it was muttering...some of it was just him chuckling. He didn't do no chuckling this morning though and it wasn't long before I heard the backdoor slam behind him...telling Grandma he had to go "Hit a lick at a snake." That meant he was going to work, but I knew he was going to check on the garden before walking up the hill to work his full day at the Pepper plant. He always walked to the plant so Grandma could keep the car for any emergency or any calling of church duties that had to be handled through the week. It didn't matter that much I suppose since the Pepper plant was just up the hill around the corner. Grandma said it was a stone's throw from the back door of everybody round there. I heard the Plant's morning whistle blow and knew that meant Grandpa was probably walking through the gates with the other plant hands.

I had no appetite for anything this morning. I just wanted my ankles to stop burning so I just laid still on the bed, waiting for Grandma's next move.

She showed up in the doorway almost like my mind willed her there. Before she could speak, a loud bang hit the front door of the porch…followed by another loud bang that came straight through the window of the bedroom. I felt a sharp sting across the brow of my left eye. I snatched my body up and felt a warmness sliding down my face and then I saw the red blood all over my britches and all over the bed pillows. Grandma pounced to the front porch door, slinging it open. One hand on the door hinge and the other reaching out towards me.

"What in the hell! What in the hell!" she screamed.

I put both hands to my face, peeping to see the same.

Another loud bang of something hit the open door Grandma was standing in, striking her on the shoulder. I fell to the floor and crawled up to her feet looking through her legs to see. There were big creek looking rocks splattered across the front porch and a woman was standing across the street in a full perch swayed back stance. Another big rock waiting to be launched. I wiped the blood from my eye trying to see through the one eye that was left clear.

"Who is it Grandma, who is that?" I whimpered.

The woman shifted to standing wide legged and launched another rock at the porch. Her hair was caught loosely at the nape of her neck. Her eyes were strangely bright and to my horror, she had a full grown beard that shaped her entire jaw.

"Grandma" I whispered, "Who is that?"

"Yo crazy ass Moma," she whispered back.

CHAPTER 4:
These Rocks Got No Names

It had been two years since I had laid eyes on Sara Lou…and it had been two years since she'd laid eyes on me. I remembered my last morning in her house- creeping from my bedroom, barefoot and clothed in my nightdress… barely tall enough to turn the doorknob that separated where I slept from the breezeway, off from Sarah Lou's bedroom, but right across from the two-cabinet kitchen.

I had trembled most of night anticipating something to happen because I had been disobedient, and it was awful waiting to be found out.

Sarah Lou had taken up with a Quartet singer, Melvin T. McGruder or as he would often say, "Melvin T for short!" He traveled through towns making concerts at whatever old Methodist church would host them. Fairbanks made space every so often at the Old County Line Church next to the black barbershop at the edge of town. They could sing and gather there and the only ones in earshot of the activity was the Old heads in line for a haircut or the lazy' s hanging around the alley pool hall.

Grandpa said he didn't trust that Melvin T. McGruder because

"He looked like a no count slickster and I ain't calling him nothing for short!" …said he didn't trust a man with a manmade handicap. Melvin T. McGruder's left side was withered and completely paralyzed so when he sang, walked, or drove…he leaned to his right.

Folks said his handicap came from another disagreeing Papa he clashed with, and a shot gun went off during the talking.
Sarah Lou did not seem to mind it. Melvin T was what they called ,"High Yeller", so Grandpa said folks looked past the rest and that was the only reason he took Lead in his Quartet of five.

It was not long upon meeting him, Sara Lou let him stay over between his Quartet travels. Grandpa said since Sarah Lou got the taste of liquor on her tongue, her mind rarely kept a sober thought. It got worse during Melvin T's quartet visits.

It was alright with me because Melvin T. McGruder brought me a Doll every time he came to town. They all did something different-from taking a bottle to whimpering "Mommy". I had collected eleven.

Sarah Lou lived amongst a group of row houses over in Buttermilk Bottom that Grandpa called "Shotgun", because he said, "you could shoot straight through the front door clear through to the back door and not touch a wall."

They stretched out in rows of ten with the back of them resting right next to the county railroad tracks. The train showing no mercy on Tuesdays and Thursdays blaring through hauling coal and blowing black smoke.

Buttermilk Bottom is what the locals called that area not far from Taylor Street. It got its name because when it rained the earth would turn milky and white and Grandpa said, "Nothing worth having was cranking out from that den of inequity."

As I crept from my bedroom that morning, I peeped from the breezeway off from Sarah Lou's bedroom and walked quietly down the planked floor. I laid wide awake throughout the night anticipating something to happen because I had latched my door earlier. Everybody knew a child was not allowed to latch no doors in grown folks' houses. It took both my hands to lock it in place and I was sure it was heard… even over the sound of rats, scratching in the walls. I waited until daybreak hoping not to be found out.

I had lingered in the breezeway … just long enough to know I would not be heard creeping by it. Sara Lou laid with her face to the door…mouth open and cheeks stained with rouge from the night smeared across her pillow. I could see Melvin T's nappy chest hair rising and falling on the other side of her as he rested on his back. His dead arm draped across his stomach. I dotted past both and didn't look back to see if they stirred. Not a soul heard me walk through Butter milk bottom that morning across the railroad tracks.

I showed up in the doorway of Grandma's kitchen and sat on the back porch until I heard somebody stirring. It was not long before I heard Grandma catch her breath through the back screen door.

I didn't move. I didn't look up.

She grabbed me and pulled me into the kitchen.

She didn't say anything…just started making biscuits.

I didn't say anything either- just watched as she kneaded the flour dough-both of us never minding my tears, making a slow quiet escape, meeting at the bottom of my chin.

Seeing Sara Lou this morning was a shock.

There was no resemblance of the woman I left sleeping two years ago. None.

This woman was wild looking, and she was mad.

"Who the hell you throwing rocks at?" Grandma yelled, crashing my mind back into what was happening before me.

"These rocks ain't got no names on em," Sara Lou yelled back, and she let one loose again.

Grandma ducked and hurried back into the bedroom, slamming the door shut. She quickly sprawled across the bed and peered out the broken window. I sprawled across too, over her elbows trying to steal a view. Everything was a mess. The bed was a mess. My face was a mess…and Grandma was a mess. Grandma wiped her hand across my head repeating, "She done had her a episode…Lord, she done had her a episode."

Sarah Lou yelled from the hedges, "Ya'll baptizing around here and nobody thought to tell me! She my child! You hear me old Lady? she snarled. "She my child not yo child!"

Grandma slid off the bed.

"She done had herself another nervous breakdown…" She whispered to herself.

Grandma eased back to the front porch door and looked over at me. The bed soiled, blood still running down my face. She put one hand over my eye and opened the door slowly with the other.

"Be real still," she said, looking back to me quietly. I tried except for my breathing which was not minding. At least I didn't hear no more rocks coming through.

"Be real still now," Grandma insisted, pressing her hand on the wound over my eye, keeping her eyes posted through the cracked door. I put my hand to my mouth to steady my breathing.

"You done bust this child head wide open! Wide the hell open! Wide the hell open! Who you throwing dem rocks at Sarah Lou?" Grandma yelled.

"I said dem rocks ain't got no names on em," Sarah Lou snapped back, spinning her head about like her neck was free of bone. Then suddenly, Sarah Lou straightened her back, dropped the rock from her throwing hand, brushed the dust off the hem of her dress and to our surprise, took off running, straight up the hill towards the Pepper Plant-like a loose dog was behind her. "Grandma?" I whimpered. "I'm still. I'm still now." To that, she looked over and pulled me to the back porch steps, right where I left the water from before…using the same pee-stained rag to wipe down my forehead. The bleeding had slowed, and Grandma said she could see the white meat of my head.

"What Grandpa gone say when he come home…and see my head bust wide the hell open?" I was crying. I knew I said a bad word, but I just did not care.

Grandma paused and with a small twinkle in her eyes, sat straight back on the porch steps, and whispered, "I suppose he'll say dem rocks… had my name on it."

CHAPTER 5:
Bringing the Bones

It had not struck Noon, so Grandpa had not made his appearance from the Pepper plant. I was sure he'd show up sooner if only to figure out why Sarah Lou sprinted out past the plant earlier early that morning. Grandma said she was sure somebody would tell him before God got the news.

The Pepper plant, as it's called, was the sole provider of employment for the whole town of Fairbanks. Everybody had a place. The white men would oversee the hiring and placement of workers. The black men would eagerly compete for the work offered daily-standing in groups each morning with their backs straight and strong. Each trying to look more capable than the other because being that and having the Boss know your worth, was what got you picked for labor every day. Grandpa's work spot was solid. It was never up to decide because his reputation of good work was already known amongst the good white folks that had anything important. His spot was permanent, but he still couldn't go as he pleased if it was outside of the clock punch time or before that whistle blew.

That whistle blaring from the Pepper Plant was indeed the work clock-each blow meant there was somewhere "You had better be," Grandpa said.

The Six am whistle meant if you were not up thirty minutes before it, you would be late, hungry and the last picked for labor, if at all. The noon whistle meant it was time for the plant workers to break for lunch. If you were lucky enough to live close by, you could dash home for smothered pork chops and gravy, a hot biscuit, and some cold iced tea…and Grandpa was lucky.

He always showed up on schedule and Grandma's job was to keep me from underfoot while he refueled to get back to the plant. Except, today, I was waiting for him so he could see what became of my head, white meat showing, blood still crusty on my brow…I was waiting for him to see it and even more eager to see what he was going to do about it.

It wasn't long before Grandpa's large frame filled the back door, his stained overalls stuffed with Prince Albert tobacco, smelling of red peppers and pickled pears and there I sat, watching. My head still throbbing. He took one look and sprang into the kitchen stumbling right into Grandma, who was stirring gravy on the stove.

"What went on now? What happened to her head?" I think

Grandpa must have asked five questions before Grandma held her spoon to his chest stopping his onslaught.

"That gal came through here after you left, and I swear… looking like a wild dog…chunking rocks…mad as hell about the baptizing…somebody must of told her. Bet you it was Deacon Otis…can't mind his damn business!"

"That gal who?" Grandpa responded. Grandma just fired him a look back as if to say…you know who!

Then all he said, for what seemed like minutes on end, was "Um hum, um hum, um hum " as Grandma recounted the details…all the while piling him up a plate of food, scoffing and making her imaginary account of Deacon Otis gossiping and bringing the bones with his storytelling. She knew Deacon Otis crossed everybody's path with his Life Insurance collecting, and money wasn't all he looked to gather. Grandma said he collected dollars and brought the bones at every stop. I knew that meant he gossiped, and Grandma always said, "Be careful of the ones that bring you the bone, cause they always take one back." Grandma looked out the back porch screen door and told me to go on and play with Mandy, so I wouldn't be in

62

grown folks' mouths.

"I'll leave you a portion for eating later on when I get back from collecting church dues." There was no room for back talk and I knew to get along like I was told. I knew also that Grandpa was going to check on Sara Lou before he went back to the plant and he wasn't going to let me go with him. I laid alongside the back kitchen wall until he threw open the kitchen screen door making his way back up the hill. I darted through the fence of honeysuckle bushes, running as low to the ground as I could so Grandpa wouldn't notice I was following. I knew not to catch up completely because he would turn me around. By the time he rounded Buttermilk Bottom to Sara Lou's front door, the Sheriff's car was already out front. I saw Grandpa quicken his step, then disappear through the door.

I crouched down beside the broken-down porch across the street. That's where Auntie Kizzy Lee lived. She ran a bootleg liquor house. Auntie Kizzie Lee was standing, leaning on the porch rails, with her dress top buttoned low. Her woman parts were dangling. She saw me but she didn't say a word. Auntie Kizzie Lee was a well-built woman, with wide hips and dangling curls. Grandma said she was top heavy like Miss Maude Smith from the Mother board. Those Ladies sat off from the right of the Pastor on Sundays and Miss Maude Smith was on the front bench, facing the deacons on the other side. Her top lady parts laid over in her lap. It was fascinating to watch when she got the Holy Ghost due to the good preaching, the ushers trying to restrain her. Several of the deacons even seemed more than willing to assist.

Auntie Kizze Lee was the middle daughter of Grandma's children, and she took a strong liking to me.

She had me on regular cleaning duties every Monday morning during the Summer after her Bootleg liquor Sunday parties when I stayed with Sara Lou.

The stench of the shot glasses doused with old cigarette butts didn't bother me none. It was the roaches and rats that made the cleanup a long haul. I had figured out that banging on bar top first would get them to scatter before I started my cleaning. I never spoke about the cleaning to Grandma caused she had little good to say about Aunt Kizzie Lee's bootlegging business. I liked helping Aunt Kizzie Lee. It was an easy three dollars and fifty cents. I liked the ways she had about herself. She'd spit out her back door all the time like it was a contest, and she moistened her legs with the chicken grease left over from Sunday night cooking. I was to pour the grease in a tin can on the stove and Aunt Kizzee would reuse it every week. First, to cook for her customers and then, grease her legs, once it cooled down.

Grandma was "shamed" of her bootlegging and everything that landed in Buttermilk Bottom, which included all three of her daughters. Aunt Kizzie Lee with her bootlegging, Sara Lou with her fast living, and Aunt Sue Mae-nobody really spelled out clearly what she did, but folks were always asking her for a root or a special remedy. I learned not to bring nothing up.
Suddenly the front door of Sara Lou's sprang open, and She was pulled across the porch by the white Sheriff and another white man to the waiting Patrol car, strapped down in a jacket that had her hands completed folded behind her back. Grandpa followed behind them, frowning, and looking like he didn't know what to do with his hands.

Aunt Kizzie Lee raised up from the porch railing and whispered, "I just be damned." I guess Sara Lou hadn't been over there asking for whiskey credit because Aunt Kizzie Lee looked like she'd seen a ghost at the sight of her bearded Sister. It seemed like everybody in Buttermilk bottom was outside, pretending to look busy but tuned into the white Sheriff's every move. It took both them white men to get Sara lou in back of that patrol car. She was bucking and thrashing about and that white sheriff was none too kind with his words.

"Settle your ass down, Gal!" He shouted. "You gone break your neck cause that jacket ain't gone give!"

"Lawd, they got the straight jacket on her," Aunt Kizzie Lee uttered. "She done had a nervous breakdown."

"Papa Leary? Ya'll alright," Aunt Kizzy Lee called out, looking over the heads of the white men.

"Look like it going like it need to," Grandpa called back.

"Ain't nobody told me nothing, Papa Leary, or I would have show come round there," Aunt Kizzie Lee responded, reaching in the waist band of her skirt, pulling out a cigarette.

Grandpa didn't look over, eyes still fixed on Sara Lou.

I sank lower next to the porch wishing Aunt Kizzie Lee would hush.

"Welp, let me know what I can do. You know Lil Lisa can still come through for a little work if needed. I ain't seen her in a while! I can always use help wiping down the kitchen," She drawled, putting the unlit cigarette in her mouth, cutting her eyes slyly towards me.

Grandpa still acted like he didn't hear, watching the Sheriff's car speed up the road with Sara Lou.

Auntie Kizzie Lee knew I was not to come over again since she said "Sara Lou showed her natural ass" at her Christmas eve bootleg party. Aunt Kizzie Lee had made a deal with the guitar player that played for Melvin T's Quartet group since they was in town anyway. He was to come over and play some blues on his guitar to kick off the party. Christmas eve was a good night of business for Aunt Kizzie Lee no matter if it fell on a Sunday or not. Most able bodied folks in the Bottom ended up there for drinks and chicken to celebrate baby Jesus. It was a drunken affair and that Christmas eve with the guitar player coming, was sure to be a treat. Aunt Kizzie Lee made one mistake that evening though. She invited me to clean but she never got around to telling Sara Lou about the party. Sara Lou didn't mind me cleaning but not getting a special howdy on the invite did not sit well with her. It did not sit well at all.

I had just finished the cleaning of the kitchen when the guitar player arrived. He set up quickly in the living room- strumming blues that spoke of drunk women and heartbreak- far removed from the gospel tunes he normally stuck to in the quartet band. The room was filling up with grinning men and women folks, some stopping in just for a shot of whiskey and some settling in waiting on Santa Claus. I was trying to make my way to the door when it suddenly swung open almost hitting me in the face. There stood Sara Lou, dressed in red, from head to toe, looking around with a fake surprised beaming expression. She ignored me, and threw her arms wide and shouted, "LIVE BAND!" … then she threw open her red silk blouse, exposing a heaving mess of caught up breast meat in a torn cotton bra.

Again, she yelled, "LIVE BAND!", this time spinning around until she was full frontal in the middle of the living room, "LIVE BAND!", She shouted again, laughing like a snarling hyena, then she delivered her final blow with an accusation she shouted towards Aunt Kizzie Lee…

"AND YOU DIDN'T INVITE ME!"

To this the crowd and guitar player joined her in laughter as Sara Lou bounced and gyrated to her yelps of "YOU DIDN'T INVITE ME!" and as the crowd of drunken folks joined in the cheer. Aunt Kizzie Lee pushed me through the door behind the gyrating Sara Lou, cursing and huffing. Aunt Kizzie Lee was mad…Sara Lou was mad…and I was ashamed. Sara Lou banned me from my bootleg house cleaning job and said Aunt Kizzie's boys can clean up after the drunkards. Aunt Kizzie Lee said the pot can't call the kettle black and she never had me around since.

My mind went back to the scene Sara Lou was making. It was yet another performance for Buttermilk Bottom. This time she was not drunk but stark raving crazy.

Me and Aunt Kizzie lee watched Grandpa set off blindly up the street like he was following the police car, but I knew he had to make his way back to the Pepper Plant because that Plant whistle was blaring something awful…breaking up the

Buttermilk Bottom play act. I could see Aunt Sue Mae up the street watching, but she never left her porch chair. You would have thought we were no kin at all.

I knew it was time for me to go back home, but the moment I went to rise, I saw a movement from the side of Sara Lou's row house. He stepped out with his maroon brim hat in his right hand and with his matching three-piece suit-His eyes taking in all of Aunt Kizzie Lee, who went back to leaning on her porch rails. I could see that left hand flopping to his thigh, like dead weight on a maimed animal.

It was Melvin T. McGruder, and my legs got weak.

He stepped into the street and looked up at the road watching Grandpa. That's when my legs came to life, and I did what I do best. I ran.

I didn't stop until I reached the outside of Grandpa's garden. Grandma hadn't left the house yet and parked in driveway was Mr. Tyron Bee's Gypsy cab. He was the only cab driver for the colored folks, so he always had good business going except Grandpa didn't allow him around our place when he wasn't there, but there he was. Mr. Tyron Bee was "fresh" I didn't want to take any chances with Grandma figuring out what I had been up to. The whole morning was off. Nobody was doing anything like they were supposed to, so I ran off to the Jones place across the string bean patch to meet up with Mandy.

The creek was so low this day I could step across it in six swoops. Mandy stood at the top of the embankment. Her stomach protruding over the waist of her britches. She wore britches all the time. She said it was because she had to help around the place and a dress was in the way. I think it was because her stomach was too big for the belt that came with the dresses.

"Hey gurl," I chirped.

"Hey gurl," she chirped back and went back to sprawl across the porch steps. My forehead was thumping, and flies were starting to swarm around my head.

"What you done done to yourself?" She said, sitting up, eyeing my forehead through the shade of her raised hand.

"My Ma went crazy and She came over and threw rocks at the

porch and one caught me dead in the head."

Mandy leaned in looking, "For sho?" She asked.

"For sho," I said, running my hand across my brow.

"Well, no matter," she said, returning to her sprawl.

"My Ma said yo Ma ain't got the sense God give a billy goat," she drawled.

That made me mad. It did not stop Mandy.

"Said she was always trouble and they had to rope her to get her to school."

That made me madder.

It seemed like both Deacon Otis and his wife, Mrs. Jones, brought bones or else how would Mandy know all of this, is what I thought.

"Where were you Sunday after service," I said, changing the

subject.

"I was sleep on the back seat floor of the car," Mandy replied slyly.

"Sleep that quick?" I knew she had more to say.

She raised up and leaned in towards me whispering, "Pops keeps his hooch under the seat and since I was waiting so long…and nobody was around…"

"You didn't," I said.

"I had me a swig of it," Mandy drawled, rolling back across the porch.

"He don't know no different. It taste like strong plum droppings anyway but, it put me right to sleep."

"You didn't," I said again.

"Right to sleep I went. I didn't hear Ma and didn't hear Pa.

Hell they left me lay there til dark anyhow," She sneered. "Ma say I'm too big to be hauling and my ass would wake up when the heat hit me. It hit me…and I did."

I loved the way bad words just rolled off Mandy's tongue, like hot syrup on a cold biscuit, fascinating.

"You got black berries today?" I asked. Mandy always had food around. Sometimes blackberries, sometimes mill cookies, or even hard candy, her Ma was known for baking and gathering.

"Hell nah, but you can help me pick some."

"Talking bout the same patch down the way?"

"Yep, hell them berries almost falling off the vines. Only saw one green snake too and that's nothing if you think about the last time."

I froze at the work snake.

"I ain't going round no snakes. That's the devil on its belly." I had heard that story too many times in Sunday school.

"Ah, it's just a damn snake. Don't even bite," Mandy quipped. "Did I say I minded something biting?" I recoiled, looking at Mandy and her big stomach. She feared nothing. Especially if it stood in the way of food.

"Well, if you too scared to pick berries, we may as well pick bugs off your Grandpa's cabbage and see if we can find a ripe tomato or two." It seemed like a grand idea except I really had a taste for those berries. I remembered the canned peaches Grandma kept under her bed. They were only brought out during the winter when snow made it impossible to get to the store. Those peach preserves over hot biscuits were like heaven in a plate.
"I know where we can get some preserves." I could not believe I volunteered the information. Mandy hung on every word following.

"Where?"

I hesitated, knowing there would be a point of no return.

"Follow me."

I led her back across the creek and Mandy took the six steps without issue. We stalked through the garden, kicking aimlessly at the cabbage leafs only half interested in the worms that laid about. I was sure Grandpa was still off trying to make sense of what the Sheriff was gone do with Sara Lou. I walked quickly to the bedroom doorway with Mandy on my footheels.

"Stay here," I demanded, trying to keep her in the open doorway. I crept across the room and reached under the bed until my hand settled on the cool jar with hard ridges across the top. I pulled the jar to the light and turned to find a smiling Mandy. "It's gone be hell opening that jar, but I know a secret,"

She snickered, yanking the jar from my hand, bolting to the kitchen sink. Standing on tip toe, she held the jar under steaming water. The top popped off effortlessly and the sweet yellow peaches rose to the top. I scooped my hand in the jar and Mandy did likewise. We had our fill of half the contents when I heard feet approaching.

"That's Grandma," I whispered, scared to death.

"Shit now, put the jar in the cabinet and hush," Mandy wailed. Grandma came into the kitchen, finding us both perched,

Christian-like, at the table, hands folded tightly in our laps. Grandma removed her scarf from her head. It was filled with the colors of a full-grown Peacock-hues of red, blue, yellow, and such. It faired oddly with her deep skin tone and bled into the sweat that was running down her face.

"Hey Mandy, nice britches." That was Grandma's way of speaking and spitting at her at the same time.

"Hey Mrs. Leary, nice bonnet." That was Mandy's way of spitting right back.

Grandma placed her kerchief of money collected and notebook at the kitchen table moving at a snail pace. I rose to move towards the door, hoping Mandy would follow.

"Hey gurl," the words stopped me at the screen door.

"I said, Hey gurl," Mandy repeated, commanding attention. I turned to look at her. Grandma followed suit.

"Wasn't that good," she said, drooling.

I gave her a blank stare.

"You know," she said, flopping from the kitchen chair, exposing her stomach, drenched in peach juice.

"That what we had a while ago." It was at that moment I felt pure hatred. I hated being scared…hated feeling breathless… but mostly hated big stomach Mandy. I watched her as she marched out the door. I could see her in my mind as she scampered through the green beans down the embankment to her side of the creek. All the while the peach juice ran from the cabinet bottom onto the wooden countertop revealing its obvious hiding place. I must have flipped it over in my hurriedness. The sweetest treat on one of the hottest days of summer. Also, one of the worst switches I had to pick.

I ended up sitting on the front porch waiting on Grandpa to top the hill. I didn't know if he was still figuring out Sara Lou's condition or back at the Pepper plant. I was sure there would be more talking about it, but I was not to be in grown folks mouth so I had to figure out how to get the news of it. Sure enough I saw him and he didn't seem to be in no hurry to get to us so I ran out to meet him. He stopped when he saw me running and just let me jump in his arms and rifle through his pockets. I started with his chest pockets looking for hard candy that he normally kept on his person pushing past his can of Prince Albert smoking tobacco until I found the peppermint. Chuckling, he grabbed my hand as we walked towards the house. "You behaved while I was gone?"

I dropped my head and told him about big stomach Mandy, my whipping, and wiping on my head yearning for sympathy. I didn't say anything about Mr. Tyrone Bee and his gypsy cab. He grunted and said, "Looks like you wore quite a whipping today…from head to toe."

I wanted to ask about Sara Lou but thought the better of it. By the time we got to the front porch, Grandma was already standing there-hands on hips.

"Welp?" She prodded.

"They took her down to Milledgeville," Grandpa responded, pushing me into the open screen door.

"Go on and wait for me on the back porch. I need to run flowers over to the church in a lil bit for our folks."

That was getting me out of grown folks' mouth.

I knew Milledgeville, Mississippi was where they took people that went crazy. That is where they took Mr. Mack Miller one time after he fell out at Aunt Kizze Lee's from "mixing his liquors" as Aunt Kizzy Lee told it. Mr. Mack Miller was the town drunkard, and he loved to walk the streets doo-wopping a song. Grandpa said he was an old washed-up Quartet singer that gave in to the drink. We did not see him for months at a time after they sent him to Milledgeville. It made me wonder how long Sara Lou would be there. I know if Grandpa had any say it would not be long.

"Lisa, go on and get in the car and hold on to these flowers," said Grandpa, making his way towards the Chrysler. Grabbing the flowers carefully, I piled in the car with Grandpa on the front seat. The flowers were to go on the grave of Grandpa's Daddy, Clarence Leary. It was something we did every year before Church homecoming, so his grave looked dressed up. We missed this ritual this year because I was running late for the Baptism. Grandma had arranged the flowers herself from her flower garden. She tended Roses and Azaleas mostly because she said they were strong flowers and hard to kill.

This time the drive to the church was slower and I spent time taking in all that we passed.

Fairbanks, Mississippi had one big country church in the downtown area. It sat close to the road with old graves perched and lined up out front. Marble headstones towered in a staggering display of family names –The Creys, Phillips, Van Ruffins, Madison's-all boldly divided and laid out according to their death dates. The church was surrounded by old white mill town houses with the American flags blowing off the front porch. Grandpa told me those were white folks graves in front of a white folks Church.

"Us black folks put our loved ones back of the church so we could bear witness to their spirits in private," he said proudly.
We finally arrived at the dirt road turnoff, driving back through the woods towards New Hope Baptist church. It occurred to me how isolated things looked alongside the road. It was different than Homecoming Sunday and today's charge was different, which was to make sure Grandpa's Daddy, Clarence Leary,

had some flowers on his resting spot. It seemed simple enough. Grandpa said he didn't want the grave out there not looking

"Up to par."

I was told his Daddy was a man that always looked up to par. Fine suit on Sunday and crisp overalls during the rest of the week, always up to par. Much like Grandpa.

He pulled up to the Church and parked in his normal spot. The parking area was empty of worshippers. I slipped off the front seat after Grandpa stopped the car, clutching the flowers proudly.

"You go on round back there, I'll be inside clearing up a bit," he muttered.

I marched out towards the graves not looking too interested in anything but the marker for Granddaddy's Pa-Clarence Leary. His grave would be further back because that's where the older graves were. They were marked by big stones and carved out writings that were done by the undertaker or a relative with time enough to mark it... unlike the towering marble graves that were downtown with the whitefolks. I rounded the corner of the Calloway markings and was surprised to see an old green truck parked alongside the fence that surrounded that group of deceased black folks. It was not normal to see anything parked this far back of the gravesite. The truck was flat out sitting over some of the smaller tombstones. There was a hunched over man with what looked like a shovel digging around the inside fencing. I walked quietly towards the back graves and as I came closer to the back of the truck, I saw a rather stately woman straddled a small stool with her hand resting on the linked fence near the opening. I guess they didn't hear me walk up since they both jumped when I said, "Hey there! Good evening!"

"Gal, you scared me!" the woman gasped, to which the man replied, "Dot I told you I shoulda brought my pistol with me. Us back out here like this down this road by ourselves."

"Well, you don't need it for me," I snickered. "I came to just do a visit with my Grandpa's Dad, Clarence Leary. He lay right over there on the backside of this fence", pointing in that direction with my flowers.

The stately woman stood up. She was brown, hair braided

in large plaits, scattered across her broad head…like she did it herself. Grey trimmed the edges of each one. Her skin was shimmering, revealing a flawless complexion and moles sprinkled about her neck.

She walked into a gated grave compartment at the end of the fencing and threw her shoulder over the top, staring down at me…

"Who your folks?" She asked, squinting.

"My great Granddaddy was Clarence Leary," I said loudly, hoping Grandpa would hear me from the church. "His grave is…"

"Cuttin Clarence Leary?" She stepped back, cutting me off. "Yes mam!" When she said "cuttin" I knew she meant "cousin" and at that moment, I knew we were kin.

"Cuttin Clarence over there next to Cuttin Smitty, Cleo, and his sister, Aunt Lily." I already knew that, but She seemed to want to ramble on.

"Now, Cleo was married to Smitty, and she died after he did. I don't know why Cleo brought Smitty down here for burying, the way he treated her."

The man grumbled "Now Dot!" in response, all the while pruning inside the fenced grave. The chopping of grass and rocks not bothering the chatty woman one bit.

I was all lit up because of what I thought was an unexpected family finding. The woman leaned in closer, arm draping firmly over the fence. She squinted again, this time looking me up and down….

"So, Cuttin Clarence your great granddaddy, eh?" she queried.

"Yes Maam," I replied.

"That was a big man…yep…a big man," she whispered.

"You Lisa," she whispered with certainty.

I froze.

"Yes, I'm Lisa," I responded. Then she said something that made me wish I had brought a small stoop of my own to sit on.

"Ah, Let me hush…I'm talkin too much," mimicking the words of the grave prunning man.

A crooked smile spread across her face and a glint of mischief lit up her eyes.

"No, you ain't," I said quickly. "You ain't talkin too much. How did you know my name?"

She rared back and put her hands on her hips.

"I put two and two together. You looking like yo Mama…that be Sara Lou Leary, right?"

"Yes, that's her!" I said.

She smiled, but it was not a happy expression.

"Crazy Sara Lou," she muttered with a piercing stare.

"Crazy as hell. Always have been. We used to run together. But, let me hush…I'm talkin too much."

The Man agreed, hunched over the shovel muttering, "Dot, you talkin too much."

She spat back over her shoulder, "Well that what it be…just like I tole you" and turned back around to me.

"Please, you ain't talkin too much …tell me everything," I spoke.

I was excited to hear more.

The woman continued, "Sara Lou…she got pregnant, but she kept her condition a secret. I mean, or so we thought," she said, chuckling.

"Yeah, I'm talkin too much," she continued to laugh.

The shoveling man interrupted again, shaking his head, whispering, "Dot, you talkin too much."

He hunched over, deeper, digging around the graves, attacking the weeds and bugs.

The woman shrugged in disdain.

"Well that what it be…just like I tole ya!", she repeated.

The man stopped shoveling and walked nearer. He propped up His foot on the base of the shovel.

"Yeah, Sara Lou tried her best to keep you a secret. She took up with her sisters over in Buttermilk bottom and I tried to be a true friend to her but she had her mind set up to do something."
"You know your Auntie Sue Mae, don't cha?"

She waited for my nod of agreement, "She had a way of getting shed of things. Always had a cure or a curse for something," she continued.

"Now, Dot, you talkin too much," the man interrupted again and started talking as if to change the subject.

"You go on back there lil gal and do what you came to do

with your flowers. Don't pay Dot no mind," He chided.

The Woman piped in disregarding his intention.

"Yep, I'll go back there with ya," she volunteered.

This gave her the right of way to point out anything she wanted as she strolled beside me.

"Right over there is Cuttin Pete Caldwell," she said, nodding her head to the left.

"He got his wife, Ella next to him and right here in this fencing is my Mama." She leaned back proudly.

"She over at the top and my daddy lay right beside her-he died after she did, so I made sure he was placed right there… then my two brothers, Pap and Leroy." Then she said something that turned my blood cold.

"I'm standing on my spot" and stopped abruptly.

"Yeah, your Auntie Sue Mae was the one give Sara Lou that

potion to drank that was supposed to get shed of any baby mistakes."

I turned towards her, waiting to hear more.

"It would a worked too, except she took off running before It could take good. I tried to catch her but she was too quick for me even in that condition." She started picking aimlessly at her front plaits like she wanted to pick them from her scalp.

"Yep, it didn't quite take with you," she mumbled.

By this time the old, hunched over man had caught up with us. He grabbed the woman by the hand and pulled her around to him.

"You turn me loose Lewis," she snapped. "I ain't said nothing that Granddaddy of hers don't already know. Hell, that Auntie of hers done got rid of more babies than a sick rabid mother dog," she spewed.

"Now Dot, now Dot," the Man grumbled, snatching her closer

and the Woman shot back.

"Well, that what it be, just like I tole you!", she shouted over his shoulder.

The man named Lewis pushed her away, and taking my hand he walked me over to Clarence Leary's waiting grave.

I dropped to my knees to place the flowers. I couldn't see Clarence Leary's name on the grave so well because of the swelling of tears in my eyes. I looked over to the woman called Dot and muttered the only thing that came to mind.

"Don't it bother you to be standing on it…your grave…like that."

Turning, looking at me and then to the ground, Dot dragged her foot across the dirt and smiled.

"Ah who?" She laughed, throwing her head back.

"Don't bother me none where I'm standing. Least I know where I be when I die. Don't bother me none what I said either," throwing Mr. Lewis a flippant look.

I could tell it didn't bother her. She didn't seem to mind telling graveyard stories and my mind kept spinning around her words, especially the grandpa knew part. Grandpa knew... "You see that spot over down the line where Cuttin Cliff lay?" she continued, "It's clear. You can go right in there if you want to. The next time it's your time."

"For sho," I said, quietly. I had no wish to stand on or point out my own grave.

It made the hair stand on the back of my neck, so I knew it was time for me to move on. I stepped past Mr. Lewis and Ms. Dot and made my way back to the front stairs of the church to wait on Grandpa. My throat was tight and that made it painful to swallow.

It wasn't long before the old green truck started up and moved slowly down the graveled narrow road leading to the front where I sat. I couldn't see their expressions as they passed because the sun had caught my eye. I shielded them with my hand as they passed on the road in front of me and threw it up and waved.

Ms. Dot turned and waved back. Mr. Lewis kept looking straight ahead.

Grandpa walked out of the side door of the church, just as they was pulling away.

"Well, my word, who was that back off in there?"

"Ms. Dot and a man she called Mr. Lewis," I muttered.
"My God," Grandpa whispered. "Dot Caldwell and Lewis Coggins, that woman sho can talk."

"Yep", I agreed, "She sho can. She told me all about some folks buried out back."

I wanted to tell him everything she said.

"Oh yeah?" Grandpa queried.

"Ms. Dot said Sara Lou took a potion from Aunt Sue Mae and it was meant to get shed of me…and it wasn't no secret…and that you knew about it and that…,

Grandpa stopped my tirade.

"Shut yo mouth now," he snapped. "Enough of what Dot done said." He seemed annoyed. I did just that. I shut my mouth.

"A lie don't care who tell it," He snapped. He seemed real agitated about Ms. Dot and her talking.

I didn't make a peep on the drive home and I could tell Grandpa noticed but he seemed to welcome the quiet in his own way. I barely moved when he pulled in the driveway home. I didn't even notice the car stopping. My eyes remained fixed on the nothing in front of me.

"Gone and make your way to your grandma. See if she needs something done."

I opened the door of the car, scampering out the front Seat and didn't stop walking until I reached the corner of the garden. I didn't care what Grandma needed. I didn't care what Grandpa said. I wanted to be somewhere no one was. I had been brought my own bone. Grandma said, when someone brings a bone, someone takes a bone back with em.

I took mine back to my grandpa. He didn't seem to know what to do with it.

CHAPTER 6:
The Left Side of Grace

I moved from the corner of the garden and flopped down in the middle of it where Grandpa said he planted some potatoes for me. I didn't see any evidence of it, just green sprouts peeping out the ground. White Potatoes were my favorite. Grandma would fry me up a mess of them if I was especially good. This patch was special because Grandpa planted a whole row just for me. I drew my knees close under my chin, which was chattering like I'd been left out in the cold, except it was hot in the garden today. I muffled the sound of my chattering through the hem of my dress. I didn't see Grandpa until he was right up on me blocking the sun. He moved over towards the tomato vines and grabbed his garden chair placing it right up next to me. That garden chair was made so it sat real close to the ground... making us knee to knee.

Grandpa had Mr. Blind Frank make it that way on purpose. Mr. Blind Frank lived up the street in a small shack of a house by himself. He could weave a chair out of dried sugar cane strips. That's how he made his living after "going blind from catching the sugar" is what Grandpa told me. Everybody on Taylor street had a sort of them. Grandpa said he could look up from the bottom of the garden straight to the top from that view and hardly anybody knew he was out there. I placed my hand on the leg of it to draw even closer.

"Welp…now what the matter be?" He asked looking straight ahead.

"That head of yours gone clear up quicker than you know it.

Ain't nothing to worry bout."

My head was stinging and drawing garden gnats that I gave up swatting. At least I could feel something I thought. I was suddenly just so tired. I laid my head over on Grandpa's knee. My mind went back to Sarah Lou's house…back to that day I crept from it… back to that night before.

I could hear Sarah Lou snoring from the other room. It was the time of night that nothing was to move. Not even the neighborhood dogs. Except Melvin T. McGruder.

I could hear him rambling about in the kitchen. The light from the refrigerator peeped under my door. I laid on my side staring at it until the light went dark, hoping…

I heard him dragging that crippled foot as it stopped at my door and witnessed the door knob turning quietly followed by a slight push. I closed my eyes pretending. I felt the side of the bed give way. A voice close to my ear whispered," You gone fix me breakfast?" I didn't respond.

"Hey…You gone fix me breakfast?" He repeated.

My body went rigid as his working hand slid underneath the covers and rested on my stomach.

"You like your dolls, don't you?" he whispered in my ear, making my ear drums tingle. My eyelids fluttered. I loved dolls and every time Melvin T came to town, he would bring me one. I had eleven of them. They each did different things; One could wet herself ,one could grow hair, one could say Moma if you held her a certain way, all did different things and all of them were white. I was as tickled as Sarah Lou was, looking at them. "You like your dolls don't you?" The hand moved lower. I tried to respond but my voice was shut out by his wet intrusive tongue against my teeth. It smelled like cigarettes and gin. The same smell as Aunt Kizzie Lee's bootleg juke joint. I couldn't speak. I wouldn't open my eyes. This wasn't the first time. This wasn't the first night. The nights came often. Melvin T McGruder came often-always requesting breakfast- always asking about the dolls.

This night in Sara Lou's house was different. He didn't ask about breakfast, he didn't ask if I liked my dolls. He moved in silence and the giving way of the bed this night was not so gentle. I felt his full body this time…the weight of him across my body…the dead left arm draped across my neck… that working right hand…it settled past my stomach, not so gentle at all. It made me cry out in my throat. The sound was trapped there because of that smothering tongue, still dripping of gin and cigarettes. The pain shot through my lower body, and I flinched as something warm spread about my thighs. The working hand pressed upon my thigh as he lifted himself from the bed. It stopped as quickly as it started, and I was alone again. The pounding of my heart seemed to consume the dark bedroom. I lowered my hand to my thighs, and it returned to me with drips of red. I wiped it clean on the case that covered by pillow.

I slipped from the bed and reached towards the door, latching it into place…then crawled quietly back beneath the covers. I waited…then there was the light again… creeping under the door. My eyes locked on the light and then the shadow, casting a dark image, beneath the door. I saw it give way to a push, but the latch caught in its place.

What if it was Sara Lou? What if I got a whipping for locking a door in her house? What if she got mad about the mess I made on the pillow? Suddenly, the shadow retreated. I couldn't stop shaking. Pulling the covers to my chin, I waited for the first hint of daylight and slipped from the bed, leaving the dolls in a pile at the foot of it.

My mind flipped back to Grandpa. He was sitting up in his low chair and he had taken hold of my hands. I suspect because they were digging into his knee. He stared at me intensely. I looked down and saw the yellow trail of wetness that had seeped through the ground turning the potato patch a familiar hue of yellow. I couldn't believe it. This never happened during my waking hours.

"I done peed." I croaked. Lord knows I didn't want another switching.

Grandpa stood up and dragged loose dirt across the yellow trail with his boots. He turned his back to me and started talking.

"I remember sitting right chere in this garden waiting on your daddy to come through to court your moma. He came every Saturday evening. He always brought a fifth of whisky with him. I spect he was just warming me up for what was to come." He started chuckling-a strange low chuckle.

"When your moma got pregnant with you she was too scared to tell it,but I knew it was something wrong cause your daddy stopped showing up with the whisky and your moma just slinked about this garden any chance she got staying out of the way of Idell,but I could tell in my own way. I kept it to myself." He turned around to look down at my bowed head.

"I watched out for her as long as I could then she started slipping off to Buttermilk Bottom…hanging out with her sisters. Kizzie Lee and Sue Mae. I couldn't never tell them too much of nothing, they were hot as cayenne pepper! Both them left here full of baby at the same time, no husbands to boot, just full of baby. Idell just let em go. Buttermilk bottom is where they been ever since. Idell, she take on shame quietly. She poured all that shame she had right into you. Making sure she don't get a repeat of the same. That's why she keep you underfoot. Them gals laid a stench on this family, like slop on a pig. Idell only talks about it when she wants to spit at me."

Grandpa slowly sat back down.

"Sara lou had been hold up over Sue Mae for a whole month or so with her secret and then one hot day, much like this one, she came stumbling back over here. Fell flat right below them green beans," he said pointing. "I was sitting low in this garden, much like I was this day. There Sara Lou was, just sprawled out in the dirt, gagging like a poisoned dog. Gagging so bad I thought she'd never take a breath and then there you was. I didn't know what to do first, hold Sara Lou or grab you. I ran to get Idell from the house. She look like she had seen a ghost," he chuckled.

"A little black piece of a Ghost you was, Yep!"

I stared down at his boots. Grandpa didn't know what Ms. Dot had already told me. He wasn't telling his graveyard story, not even to me. I wanted to ask him if he took Sara Lou to see Auntie Sue Mae and if he knew what she was gone do? If he had taken a risk to keep from the shame? If he handled women's business, business Grandma should have been in front of. Grandma said it got by her and nothing gets by Grandma.

"Welp, we got hold of your daddy and I mean, quick," Grandpa continued.

"I sent word for him, and he met me right chere, in this garden, whisky in hand and all," he chuckled.

"I told him right to his grinning face. I says, "you done messed up my house and I want to know how you gone clean it up." He looked foolish for a minute, so I sent him to the house where Sara Lou was…lying across my bed with you at her chest." Grandpa started laughing again.

"I walked in just in time to see Idell with her apron bunched up in her hand like she wished it was a knife."

I wasn't laughing just still staring.

"That boy said, "I guess I'll marry her."

"Lord what a mess," he grunted.

"Turns out your daddy liked to gamble and well, Sara Lou liked to fight. They set up house right there in Buttermilk Bottom, right across from your bootlegging Auntie. Every weekend was a mess. She was gonna kill him one day for sho, so he left her there in the Bottom and left you with her." He turned his attention to the garden and looked over the vegetables like it was the first time he rested eyes on them.

"Child…you see them tomatoes?"

I nodded and said, yes suh.

"You see them string beans?"

I nodded.

"All that cabbage and them collards sprouting towards the light?"

I shook my head ,again acknowledging.

"Them things is reaching toward God's grace of light. They just growing out in the open for all to see. That's God's way of blessing them." He stretched his hands out.

"You see your potatoes?"

I shook my head, and said, no suh.

I didn't see no potatoes…just weedlike sprouts where they were supposed to be.

"Naw you don't do you?", Grandpa said, smiling.

He stooped and reached down into the ground beneath the green sprouts and scooped out a handful of dirt and there they were, golden, round, spotted potatoes, some small, some bigger. All clustered together like knots. I looked at his hand all filled up with them. My eyes could barely take them all in.

"You see these potatoes?"

I nodded.

"They got God's grace too. They just grow differently, in the ground, deep rooted. You don't see em sprout like them others...right out in the sun... They on the left side of God's grace. He nurturing them undercover. You can't see em. Still growing tho...still growing." He laid the potatoes at my feet.

"God can reach anything, you understand?"

I looked again at the beautiful cluster of potatoes, growed just for me.

I understood.

Then he turned to me and pulled me right into his lap. Wet dress hem and all.

"Did I get you in time?" His voice was raspy.

"Suh?" I whispered, my throat had an ache in it.

"Did I get you time?" He repeated.

I couldn't say a thing. Did he get me in time for what? Before that rock split my head to the white meat, before my daddy decided to never show up, before Sara Lou drank that liquid from Auntie Sue Mae's potion? Before Melvin T (for short) hurt me with his working hand, in time for what?

I must have been frowning something awful because Grandpa laid his big hands on both sides of my face.

"I said, "Did I get you in time?" He whispered, this time directly in my ear. I knew what he was asking, and I couldn't tell him for the first time what I knew the truth to be, so I just choked out the lie I had to tell.

"Yessum," I whispered.

"Yessum."

CHAPTER 7:
Quartet Singers Ain't Never Been No Good

Baptism Sunday had come and gone and it was like a lifetime happened in a week. The Sun was gone this Saturday and the rain came in quickly like God slung it from a bucket.

Grandma made me sit in the floor of the living room until morning came because the strorms came through so strong. I laid staring at the ceiling and didn't even know I had drifted off until I heard the front door opening and Grandma dragging a bushel through it. I had seen such a sight before and was not happy about what I knew had to be done to empty that bushel basket. It was a mess of peas and they needed to be shelled.

Grandma had already sent for Mrs. Jones to help with the shelling and she wasn't long coming through the door to help.

Grandma didn't really talk about where they came from but I heard Grandpa say one day that they must be coming from Uncle Lawrence who was off serving in the War. He was only one with an extra dime to spare and always finding a way to send something home and Grandma would send him a cake as her "Thank you." Uncle Lawrence was the youngest of the boys. Grandma told me my other Uncles left town to make more money during the planting season in Florida, because the growing season was year round there, not like it was in Fairbanks, Mississippi. All I knew was with all those peas, I had a lot of shelling to do and it had to be done fast. I sat wide legged in the floor doing my part when Mrs. Jones walked up strapping her apron on, teasing with Grandma about the task before us.

"Lord it's too hot for this but I sho preciate you letting me help out!" She knew Grandma was going to give her a portion. I didn't get an apron but a big towel to throw across my lap to capture the peas and the hulls were discarded on the side. I shelled and had to be quiet but not Mrs. Jones, she talked. A lot. One of the best things about being quiet around Grandma and Mrs. Jones was listening to Mrs. Jones carry on about everything. She was a lanky woman and would draw her dress up over her knees when she sat, making the middle part droop like a pocket, that hid her whereabouts between her legs. She had a way of talking that made you hang on her every word. She never quite finished saying what she was saying and she always ended her ramblings with "and all and everything." You just had to fill in the blanks after that.

"I knew when I seen the poster put up out front of the Old Methodist church in the alley, it was gone be some shit and all and everything."

Mrs. Jones was talking about the Quartet that was coming to town. Melvin T and his Quartet always showed up to kick off church revival or if they needed money to keep traveling commitments.

Grandma asked Why? What the poster say?, not looking up from her shelling.

"It said the MIGHTY CHRISTIAN BLUE FLAMES will be performing two nights only featuring Melvin T McGruder. He gone be leading it off… and all and everything," Mrs. Jones said, haughtily.

"Really now, what about back up's?" said Grandma, throwing pea hulls to the floor.

"Didn't mention not one of dem…and all that. Not even Mack Miller, and all that and everything," Mrs. Jones exclaimed, clutching at her chest.

"Not a word?", Grandma leaned in.

"Naw… and you know what they say about Mack Miller?" Mrs. Jones said quietly.

"What dey say?" Grandma leaned back, ignoring the peas and so was Mrs. Jones.

"Say he really had a baby by whatchamacallit," snapping her fingers trying to recall.

"Whatchamacallit, you know that live out there by the Trailway bus station and all and everything."

"Who?" Grandma queried.

"You know whatchamacallit nem—Betty Bates…her daughter Mary!", exclaimed Mrs. Jones.

"Yeah, Mary," Grandma recalled.

"That baby girl she had look just like them Mack Miller folks- nasty big lips, big ole forehead! Should a been a boy…and all that and everything," laughed Mrs. Jones.

"What?", Grandma responded, looking shocked.

"Yeah Lord, should a been a boy child and all and everything," Mrs. Jones, replied.

"Well, ain't Mary in the women's choir?", Grandma added.

"That's what I'm talking bout!" Mrs. Jones piped in excitedly. "All up in the choir like she ain't had no baby out of the wedlock, and all that and everything."

"She can sang too. That's why she ain't been sat down from the choir. Child look just like Mack folks and all that and everything!"

"I'm just thinking about that fool man, Melvin T coming back and running about with Sara Lou," Grandma interjected. "Ain't no good gone come of it. He ain't no good. Ain't met a quartet singer that was ever any good and Melvin T takes the whole cake," Grandma said, snatching the peas up like she wished it was Melvin T's throat.

"That gal already in the middle of a nervous breakdown episode. No good coming, I tell you!", said Grandma.

"They say he been here for weeks already and all that and Everything," Mrs. Jones added.

"Course you ain't heard it from me, but they say he over there laid up with Sara Lou, crazy spell and all. When I heard that, I thought die, I would! And all that and everything!"

It was dizzying to keep up with it all so I spread out even more on the floor and cupped my hands under my elbow taking it all in. I had already seen Melvin T lurking around Buttermilk Bottom the day I followed Grandpa over there. I didn't tell it though.

It didn't take long for Grandma to figure out that I had stopped shelling was just gaping in the mouth of every word Mrs. Jones was sputtering.

"Get on out here, out of grown folks' mouths!", Grandma scoffed.

I scrawled up to my feet, turning towards the back door. Grandma stopped me directing me to grab an armful of the peas, so I could continue my task on my own. I reached down to pull up as much as I could and felt something hard at the bottom of the batch. I pulled out the object and turned towards Grandma.

"Grandma, look like somebody lost a thing in this basket,"

I said, holding it high over my head.

Grandma's eyes widened and she spilled her shelled peas as she sprang to her feet.

"Lower that to your grandma, real slow baby," she said, walking towards me.

Mrs. Jones sat there with her legs still wide open.

I did as I was told and loosened it from my grip. It look like Uncle Lawrence had left more than just snap peas in that basket.

"That boy done slipped me my own pistol!" Grandma

exclaimed.

I knew a gun when I saw one. Grandpa kept one out back near the chicken shed. He used it to run off critters.

I had seen Grandma eyes twinkle over getting a new dress or pair of shoes but I never saw her eyes light up like this.

"Now, it won't be no mentioning of this...to nobody," Grandma eyes swept to me and Mrs. Jones.

"and I mean nobody."

That was going to be hard for me because that meant I couldn't tell Grandpa. I finished my pea shelling on the back porch and it wasn't long before Mrs. Jones was making her way out the door with her own mess of peas gathered in her Apron. I took that as my go ahead on going back in the house with my finishings. Grandma was getting the stove ready to start up a batch so I moved off to the middle room to look out the window while she hummed and cooked. She sure was happy to get that gun we couldn't speak about. I never heard her so happy to cook peas in my life.

"Doooo ruuuuupe!"

I heard the sound coming from the top of the hill. I pulled the curtains back further to see. It was Mr. Mack Miller. He walked the neighborhood every Saturday afternoon singing his song.

"Dooo rupe!"

The song was mimicking an old swaying quartet tune from the Mighty Christian Blue Flames opening song. Mr. Mack Miller sang it every Saturday aternoon. Grandpa said he "drove his self crazy from singing in that quartet group."

"That Mack Miller thought he was gone be lead, but that high yeller, Melvin T took over and Mack mixed liquor and failure and lost his mind."

I stood in the dining room window watching him like most Saturdays. He would circle the block and stagger his tune along with his steps.

I peered from the window, looking at his descent from the top of hill as he stumbled and sang.

"Dooooo ruuuupe!"

He was stumbling, spinning, and dipping. Grandma heard him too and quickly came into the room to tell me to hush so he would pass on by like he always did. I just peeped and watched. I put my hand to my brow and scratched a little at the scab that was forming. A nice reminder of the whipping and rock throwing that came the week before. Grandma and Grandpa seemed to have calmed down from all of it, so I responded in kind.

"Dooooo ruuuupe!"

Mr. Mack Miller was right at our front porch now and circling towards the window where I was planted. I was glad to stand there amongst the curtains anyway because the only time I came in the dining room was to dust off the bottom shelves of the old dining table before the Sunday Pastor Surry was coming to dinner.

"Dooooo ruuuuuupe!"

The sound came closer now and for some reason this Saturday

Mr. Mack Miller was giving us special attention. He never left the street with his Dooo ruping but here he was, right in our driveway, stumbling, singing, and dipping.

Grandma walked into the room and peeped out the curtains over my head. "Be real quiet…he leave off."

She walked back into the kitchen expectant of my obedience. I peered through the curtains again and before I knew it I heard,

"Dooo rupe out this yard!"

It was me.

I don't know what made me say it. It spilled out like an over filled glass of water. Well, Mr. Mack Miller was ripe from the drinking, and he quickly stumbled over to the window addressing my call. "Dooo ruuuuuupe…Dooooooo Ruuuuuupe…Dooooo Ruuuuuuupe!"

It was like he was not going to stop. Grandma slid up to me and placed a firm hand over my mouth.

"I told you to not say a thing!", she said angrily.

Mr. Mack Miller dooooo ruuuuped until he got tired.

Grandma said Mr. Mack Miller was drunk. He got stirred up from the quartet that was coming to town and he wasn't gone be the only one stirred up. I already knew it would be Sara Lou. Grandma and Mrs. Jones had already been talking. I had already been listening, getting in grown folks' mouths.

Weeks went by and word got out that Sarah Lou was home. Grandpa kept us updated as best he could about how she was fairing but Grandma said she figured it was time for her to make a move and go see for herself. Before she could make her move, Aunt Kizzie Lee made a rare appearance after we got from church and told Grandpa and Grandma what she was dealing with in Buttermilk Bottom.

"I'm doing the best I can but he just whipping her ass, excuse me for cussing," exclaimed Aunt Kizzie.

"She a fighter but they just beating the hell out of each other now." I knew who she was talking about. It was Melvin T. He was powerful with that one arm and working hand but Sara Lou was not a fair fighter. Everybody in Buttermilk Bottom knew that. There was one story told of how she slit a woman across the face because she called her out of her name. Folks said Sara Lou caught the woman in the path and pushed her from the back after she watched her get drunk at Aunt Kizzie's house late one Sunday evening. Grandma said she never seen so much blood.

"He done threw her through a damn wall in her house, excuse me for cussing, now Mama Leary, I got business to tend to and this fighting is making a show for the public to see. Sara Lou keep saying git him befo she kill him," wailed Aunt Kizzie Lee. "Somebody need to do something, Mama Leary, before we have us another mess white folks got to clean up!", she continued.
It was an unspoken rule that you never called the white police. You left that to nervous white folks. White folks only got nervous if you brought trouble too close to their door and when Sara Lou went crazy, she didn't care whose back yard she ran through. Aunt Kizzie Lee was no match for Sara Lou and Grandma knew it. Only one person was.

Aunt Kizzie Lee finally left with all her fussing about Sara Lou.

She had made her point this Sunday and she knew it was time to get back to her business…bootlegging.

Grandma left the bed that night and she did nothing about me following her. She said nothing to Grandpa who was quiet in the back. We wrapped up and slid quietly out the front porch door. I walked closely beside her as we walked up Taylor Street and rounded the corner to Buttermilk Bottom. We walked between the row houses quietly until she crept up the steps of the shotgun house where Sara Lou lived. I kept up as best I could with Grandma because her strides were wider than normal and the streets were slushy. It had stormed the night before so the ground was real milky. Grandma gave a quiet tap and to my surprise Aunt Kizzie Lee let us in. I could tell she had been sleeping on the front room couch and beckoned for Grandma to take it but Grandma moved past it and settled in the chair. Aunt Kizzie looked and me and did a shush finger across her lips as she slipped out the doorway. I wasn't about to say a word because no one else was speaking. I could hear Sara Lou snoring from her room. Grandma shifted her body to lay sideways in the chair and I found a spot on the floor beneath her. Never minding the discomfort of the hard planked floor. I didn't feel this was a night for sleeping although after about an hour I drifted off.

I didn't hear the noise at the front window but I did feel Grandma move. I opened my eyes to see her shift from the chair and walk over to the window.

Then I saw the shadow outside the window frame-the moon illuminating it. Grandma stood alongside the window. I heard the window creak like it was being tested from the other side-pushing against it. I saw the shadow move away drawing towards the second window. Grandma was already stationed at it-her body still alongside so she could not be seen. The same pressing creak came from the other side. I sat up slowly and she looked keenly at me-so much so I could see her eyes through the darkness. She moved to the middle room where Sara lou lay sleeping. The light from the window dimmed by a drapping sheet substituting for a curtain. Grandma rested her body next to the window again. I had attached myself to her thigh by now-clinging to her housedress. The shadow outside once again causing the window to creak.

Finally, Grandma moved to the kitchen. She made a quick move to the latched kitchen door, dislodging me, and she simply undid the lock. She laid her back against the refrigerator door and I reattached myself to her thigh. I could see just enough to bear witness to the door knob turning. This time something pushed open the door. It was Melvin T's working hand.

He stepped into the kitchen following it, dripping mud from his fine shoes on the floor. Grandma waited until he came all the way inside...then I saw her right hand.

I had seen that hand wring necks of chicken, roll biscuits in lard, chop wood for the fireplace. I never thought I'd see it holding this thing again. It was that pearl handled gun from the bushel of peas.

Then came a loud pop and I saw Melvin T's working hand explode with blood. It splattered across the refrigerator onto the wood kitchen floor. He stumbled backwards and fell off the back porch onto the ground below. Grandma followed him just as silently as she did from the windows, but not me... I couldn't move from the open door. She lifted the gun and hovered it over his head and Melvin T started wailing, lifting that blood dripping working hand up to his forehead. I felt something push me out of the way and dash past me to Grandma. It was Auntie

Sue Mae.

"Gimme the gun, Ma. It's enough now," She shushed, holding both hands towards Grandma.

"It's enough now," she implored.

Grandma looked skyward and tucked the pearl object down the front of her house dress. She walked back up the steps, pushing Auntie Sue Mae to the side and climbed up the back stairs to me. She didn't say a word, but I knew how to follow her.

"Take that trash out," she muttered to Aunt Sue Mae, over her shoulders, before disappearing back into the kitchen. I knew Aunt Sue Mae would know what to do. She knew how to fix anything. We walked past Sara Lou's bedroom, who was still sleeping like nothing had happened. Grandma and I walked back to Taylor Street, as quietly like we left. The sun had not come up yet and old rooster Joe was still silent. I watched Grandma get herself set for bed, so I did the same. She settled on the edge of the bed and I crawled in behind her, towards the window, my usual spot. I stared out the window until that Rooster crowed, and I heard Grandpa stirring. He was the only one moving around this morning. I waited until I heard him pull back the curtains to the bedroom.

"Idell?" He sounded confused.

"Grandma not feeling so good this morning, Grandpa. I'll lay here with her until you get back," I said.

"Idell?" He said again. I guess he wanted to hear it from her. Grandma didn't answer him and she didn't move. I guess Grandpa was going to have to make his own breakfast fixing this morning. After what seemed like forever, he moved away from the bedroom opening.

"Welp, I got to go hit a lick at a snake," he grunted, walking past the bed, out the door. He paused looking back through the window catching my eye. I stared back at him, giving him the signal to keep going, with a slow blink.

It was hours before Grandma got up and when she did, I stayed underfoot. There was no talking as she moved about the kitchen. She was getting ready to bake and only opened her mouth for tasting.

"Grandma, what cha eating?"

I had sprawled under the bottom of the kitchen table playing with the chairs, looking up as she mixed a bowl of cake batter. She would dip her finger in it from time to time as she tested her vanilla seasoning with sugar and milk, like she was waiting on the right time to stop sprinkling.

"Grandma what cha eating?" I repeated.

She paid me no mind as she kept stirring and dipping.

"Grandma?"

I couldn't figure out no other way for her to make notice of me. She hadn't been the same since last night at Buttermilk Bottom. "Grandma, what cha eating?" I pressed again, squirming on the floor of the kitchen, "A little piece of dog ass!" she responded in frustration. I stopped squirming and looked up to see her holding the spoon in hand to her forehead. She looked tired. "Give me a little piece of that dog ass," I whispered.

To that, she finally looked under the table and started to laugh.

She laughed so hard she grabbed herself between the legs and collapsed to the floor beside me. She was laughing so I started laughing. I didn't know if it was because I repeated a bad word or if it was because she had no other emotion to share.

"You do me good Lisa. You got your way about cha. You do me good," Grandma whispered.

I figured she needed me to say something to stop that dipping in the cake batter.

The footsteps at the back door brought Grandma to her feet and I rolled over from under the table to open the screened door. It was Aunt Sue Mae. Standing wide with her hair toppled on her head and a small balled up handkerchief in her hand. She walked through the door and pushed me out to the porch. I guess she had more to say about last night. I didn't move too far from the porch screen door because I knew something was about to be said.

"Where'd you get that gun," Auntie Sue Mae blurted out.

I wanted to shout out, "It came out of the Bushel of peas!" but my piping up was not needed or welcomed.

"Never mind that," Grandma responded.

"Never mind that?" Auntie Sue Mae exclaimed.

"You done shot a grown man, maimed him, about to leave him for dead wasn't for me and you gone nevermind it? I should have stopped you when I saw you round Butter Milk Bottom so late in the evening like that. I saw you from my porch but you didn't even look my way. I thought I was having a Hank sighting- an old woman and a little girl creeping that way at night. I stayed up and watched. Then I saw it, Melvin T McGruder on the prowl, like a dog that's been put out of his pen." She started shaking her head.

"I said, where'd you get it?" Aunt Sue Mae said again.

"I sent word through Tyrone Bee weeks ago. He got word to Lawrence unit and it came with his package he sent."

Auntie Sue Mae looked concerned at hearing Tyrone Bee's name come up.

"That Man ain't suppose to be coming round here Ma and you know it. Papa Leary don't like the way he looks at you and Lawrence got better things to tend to in that military then smuggling you weapons."

"Didn't nobody see Tyrone Bee. I saw to that."

Except me, I wanted to say, but again, no one needed me to pipe in. I saw that gypsy cab parked outside the back door the day I followed Grandpa. I thought it strange then.

"I knew it was the timing for me to do something. That Melvin T is the cause of Lil Lisa leaving that house. I know it… Little thing come sliding through here that morning, tears streaming, clothes stained, shaking like a leaf on a tree," Grandma groaned. "All I could do was stare at a cooking pot with a damn knot in my throat," She whispered.

"Here he come back like a bad demon, beating on Sara Lou. No Siree, it was already enough. It was my timing to do something, and I did!"

Aunt Sue Mae said nothing for a minute. It was as if she agreed.

"You don't wanna know how he's fairing," she said, as she sat down across from Grandma.

"You don't wanna know what become of his hand?" She continued.

"How's he fairing? What become of his hand?" Grandma responded back, emotionless.

"I saved it but it won't be much use. It won't hold a grip. Good thang he don't need it for his sanging and it sho won't be whipping Sue Mae ass no more. Excuse my tongue Ma," said Sue Mae, respectfully.

"Didn't see no cause to get the white folks involved ,so I fixed it as best I could until he could get across state lines anyways. He got folks somewhere ,so I expect they can take it from there. You tell Papa Leary what cha done?"

"He'll get the bone soon enough," responded Grandma, as she poured her batter in the warm greased cake pan.

"Well, it won't come from me, no maam," Auntie Sue Mae

huffed, laying the balled-up handkerchief on the table.

"Take that out of here. I don't want no parts of your rooting," said Grandma.

"Ah, you got me wrong Ma. That ain't no root. That's just a little guarantee in the making is all. Just a little of ole Melvin T's blood to dash around. It will make sure of the "No Mo's," she said, slyly.

Grandma looked confused.

"No mo quartet singing. No mo beatings. No mo Melvin T for short, coming round," Aunt Sue Mae said fiercely.

I could see the handkerchief clearly now, because I was all but pressed against the screen back door- White and stained red.

I heard footsteps behind me and I didn't need to turn around to know who it was. I recognized her breathing.

There she stood… Sara Lou, out of breath, like she had been running. It seemed like everybody was paying a visit this morning.

She looked different standing there this time. No beard, no wild look in her eyes. She stood up tall and straight with her arms folded in front of her, heaving.

She looked at me like she was looking through me, before pushing me aside to join Grandma and Aunt Sue Mae in the kitchen. She gave no morning "Howdy's", just blurted out the worst thing anybody wanted to hear.

"I'm pregnant," she drawled. The words hung in the air like pig stench in a slop pen.

Grandma stood still, eyes not lifting from the table.
Aunt Sue Mae drew the blood-stained handkerchief into her fist.

Sara Lou stepped backwards out of the door, down the steps and walked slowly up the dirt road of Taylor Street. My eyes followed her until she got out of sight.

Grandma finally lifted her head and stared at Auntie Sue Mae who slid from her chair with the balled-up handkerchief in her fist and moved towards the door causing me to scoot to the steps, where she hovered over me.

"Welp, she said she didn't want you anyways, child," looking down at my bowed head. Suddenly she knelt down to my face and pulled at my pigtail.

"Shit, she said you is black, nappy headed, got knock knees, and ashy. Now that's a damn thang to say bout your own child. Yo Mama got a meanness in her... but Ma Leary, she sho worked with you didn't she?", pulling my pigtail until I looked up. Then she threw the handkerchief under the steps below my feet, slipped off her right shoe, and kicked dirt over it with her bare foot.

"It's Ok if that be so," I muttered, watching her set her spell.

Yes, it was ok if it all be so, I thought.

"Now, don't you let nothing move that until you hear from me," Aunt Sue Mae directed, as she moved from the steps.

"It's gone keep the shadows out your door… from now on." She spat over her shoulder. Those words made me sit up straight. How did she know about the shadows? Folks were right- Aunt Sue Mae had a potion for everything.

I watched her as she swayed up the road, her hands laid to her back like it was assisting with her stride. She had an attitude about her like she was about to do something. I watched her, and I knew what she was set to do. She was following Sara Lou. I looked back at the screen door where Grandma was standing.

She was watching too.

Something felt different.

I didn't feel no trail of yellow wetness seeping from me at all. I didn't even tremble. Grandpa told me in good fashion what side I was on with God. I didn't need to take that bone Ms. Dot gave me nowhere now…cause Aunt Sue Mae just brought the bone to me. I didn't even need no blood-stained potion to keep Melvin T away, I thought, pleasingly because I had Grandma now…and Grandma, well, she had something more powerful than I had ever seen. More powerful than Melvin T, more powerful than Aunt Sue Mae spells...

She had a gun!

Made in the USA
Columbia, SC
29 July 2025